This book belongs to

_____

Intro to PHYSICS
for Babies

Copyright © 2021 by Callisto Publishing LLC
Cover and internal design © 2021 by Callisto Publishing LLC
Illustrations © 2020 Ekaterina Trukhan
Author photo courtesy of Lillian M. Ortiz
Interior and Cover Designer: Angela Navarra
Art Producer: Hannah Dickerson
Editor: Jeanine Le Ny
Production Editor: Jenna Dutton

Callisto Kids and the colophon are registered trademarks of Callisto Publishing LLC.

All rights reserved. No part of this book may be reproduced in any form or by any electronic or mechanical means including information storage and retrieval systems—except in the case of brief quotations embodied in critical articles or reviews—without permission in writing from its publisher, Sourcebooks LLC.

All brand names and product names used in this book are trademarks, registered trademarks, or trade names of their respective holders. Callisto Publishing is not associated with any product or vendor in this book.

Published by Callisto Publishing LLC C/O Sourcebooks LLC
P.O. Box 4410, Naperville, Illinois 60567-4410
(630) 961-3900
callistopublishing.com

Printed in the United States of America.

Intro to PHYSICS for Babies

A PUPPY IN MOTION TENDS TO STAY IN MOTION...

Charles Liu

Illustrations by Ekaterina Trukhan

callisto publishing
an imprint of Sourcebooks

Dear Parents and Caregivers,

Little kids love learning science! Every time they toss a toy, swing in a swing, or even fling a fork, they're exploring the laws of physics. It's never too early to bring science to young children; all we have to do is encourage their natural curiosity and love of play. However, breaking down complicated topics so that they're understandable isn't easy. I wrote this book for all of us who want to teach little kids about science in a fun and engaging way.

Intro to Physics for Babies presents Isaac Newton's famous three laws of motion, as well as his law of universal gravitation, through a playful story about friendship and teamwork. At the end of the book, I've included a handy tip sheet for adults to help explain these physics concepts in further detail to extra-curious kids.

I wish your child joy and delight in reading this book—and learning about the basis of modern physics, too!

Sincerely,
Charles Liu

The Law of
INERTIA

It's morning!
The puppy is ready to play.

But a kitty at rest tends to stay at rest . . .

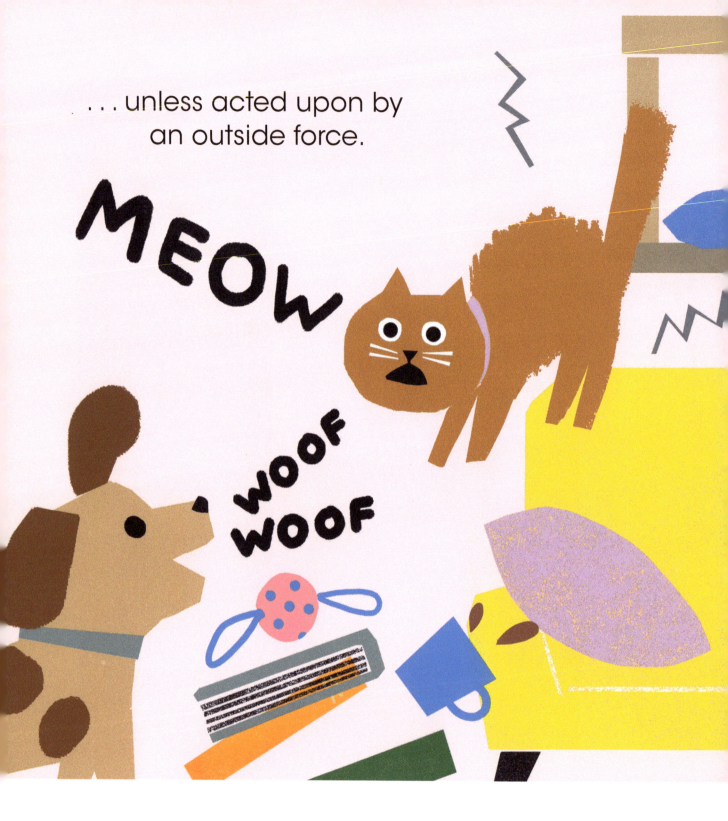

And a puppy in motion

The Law of
FORCE

A force can be a pull or a push.

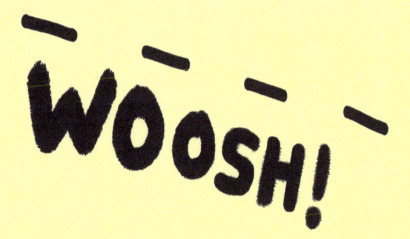

Force changes the speed of motion . . .

...and the direction of motion.

If there is no motion, there is no net force.

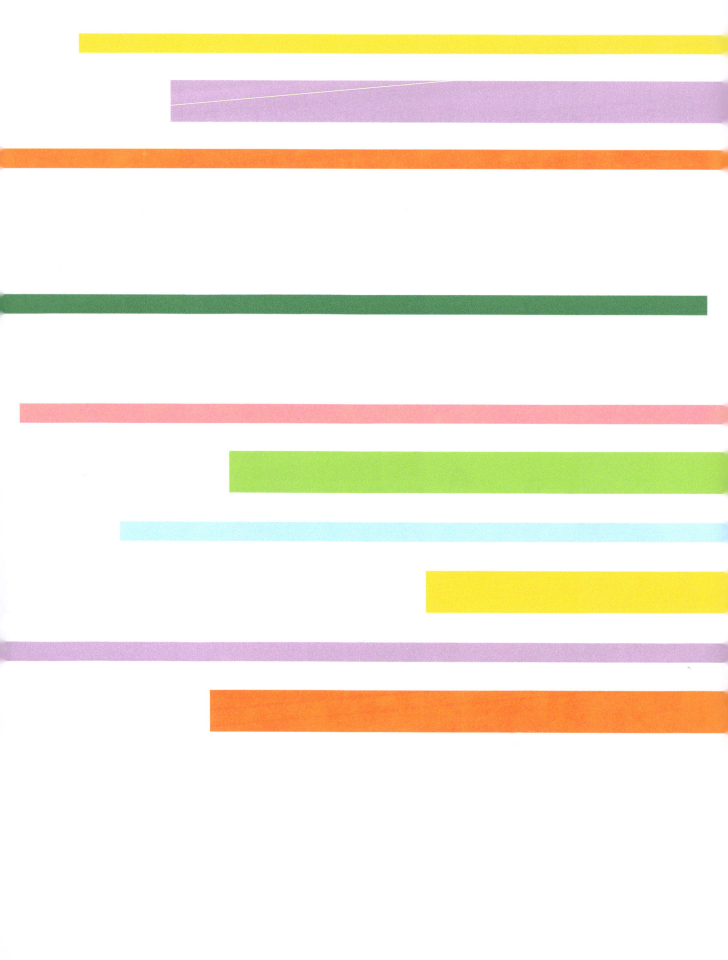

The Law of REACTION

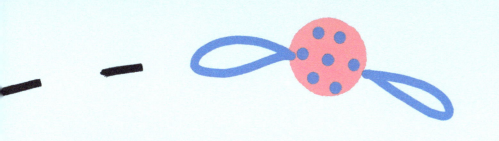

Force causes actions.

For every action

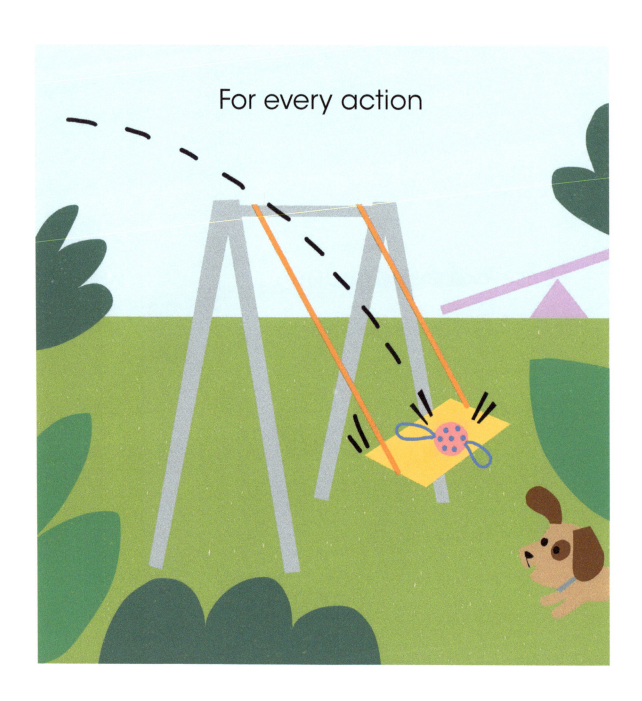

there is a reaction.

Reactions are equal and opposite.

The Law of
UNIVERSAL GRAVITATION

When a puppy jumps up,

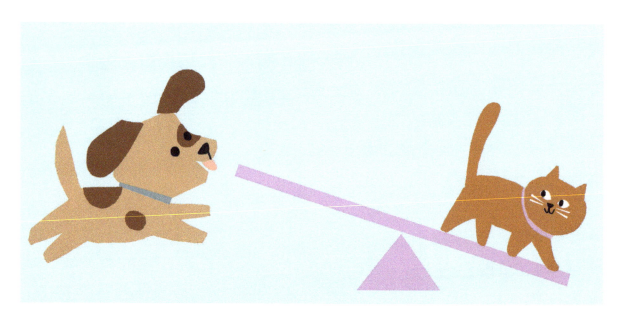

Force is greater when mass is greater.

It's also greater when a kitty speeds up.

But Earth has more mass than kitties or puppies.

So, Earth's force of gravity pulls the kitty down to the ground, too.

It's what keeps puppies and kitties on a comfy couch, dreaming, instead of drifting up into space.

What a wonderful day! They are at rest.

Intro to PHYSICS
(for Adults)

The English scientist and mathematician Isaac Newton developed three famous laws of motion that form the basis of physics today.

The Law of Inertia (in-UR-sha): If an object (or a kitty or puppy) is at rest, it won't move unless an outside force causes it to move. In the same way, an object in motion will stay moving in a straight line and without changing speed, unless an outside force causes it to change direction or speed.

The Law of Force: How do we calculate what happens to an object when an outside force gets involved? The amount of force an object feels is equal to the object's mass multiplied by the acceleration the object feels. As an equation, this law is commonly written as $F = ma$. In physics, acceleration can be positive (speeding up) or negative (slowing down), so a force can also be positive (a push) or negative (a pull). The more massive an object is, the more force it takes to accelerate it.

The Law of Action and Reaction: For every action, there is an equal and opposite reaction. If one thing pushes another thing, that other thing automatically pushes back just as much, and in the opposite direction. That's why, when ice skaters push against one another while facing each other, they both go backward.

Isaac Newton also discovered another law of physics.

The Law of Universal Gravitation: Gravity, which causes objects to move toward one another, can be described as a pulling force. The pull of gravity is stronger if the masses of the objects are larger, and the pull is weaker if the distance between the objects is greater. When the forces on an object exactly balance the gravity it feels, then the object is temporarily weightless. That's what happens when astronauts seem to float around in space—they still have mass, but they're in orbit around Earth, and so they are weightless.

About the Author

CHARLES LIU is a professor of physics and astronomy at the City of New York's College of Staten Island and an associate with the Department of Astrophysics and Hayden Planetarium at the American Museum of Natural History. He and his wife have three wonderful children who love learning about science.

About the Illustrator

EKATERINA TRUKHAN is a Russian illustrator, children's book author, and designer. She likes to create cheerful work to make people smile. Her work is inspired by vintage children's books, mid-century design, and everyday life.

Printed in the USA
CPSIA information can be obtained
at www.ICGtesting.com
LVHW072153091224
798742LV00050B/2433